IN THE POCKET

A 2014 *WASHINGTON POST* ARTICLE SAID: "PRESCOTT MAKES YOU WANT TO JOIN THE TEAM AND DO WHATEVER HE SAYS."

FAMILY TIES

Rayne Dakota "Dak" Prescott was born on July 29, 1993. He grew up in Louisiana with his mom, Peggy, and two older brothers, Jace and Tad. His dad's name is Nathaniel.

IN THE POCKET

PRESCOTT'S BROTHER JACE MADE HIM WANT TO PLAY FOOTBALL.

GAME-CHANGING QUARTERBACKS

DAK PRESCOTT

Gareth Stevens Publishing

HOT TOPICS

BY P. J. FREEDMAN

Please visit our website, www.garethstevens.com. For a free color catalog of all our high-quality books, call toll free 1-800-542-2595 or fax 1-877-542-2596.

Library of Congress Cataloging-in-Publication Data

Library of Congress Cataloging-in-Publication Data

Names: Freedman, P. J., author.
Title: Dak Prescott / P.J. Freedman.
Description: Buffalo, New York : Gareth Stevens Publishing, 2026. | Series: Game-changing quarterbacks | Includes bibliographical references and index.
Identifiers: LCCN 2024052759 (print) | LCCN 2024052760 (ebook) | ISBN 9781482472448 (hardcover) | ISBN 9781482472431 (paperback) | ISBN 9781482472455 (ebook)
Subjects: LCSH: Prescott, Dak–Juvenile literature. | Football players–United States–Biography–Juvenile literature. | Quarterbacks (Football)–United States–Biography–Juvenile literature.
Classification: LCC GV939.P74 F744 2026 (print) | LCC GV939.P74 (ebook) | DDC 796.332092 [B]–dc23/eng/20241208
LC record available at https://lccn.loc.gov/2024052759
LC ebook record available at https://lccn.loc.gov/2024052760

Published in 2026 by
Gareth Stevens Publishing
2544 Clinton Street
Buffalo, NY 14224

Cover Designer: Nicholas Switalski
Interior Designer: Rachel Rising
Editor: Kristen Nelson

Photo credits: Cover, p. 1 NurPhoto SRL / Alamy Stock Photo; Back Cover, EFKS/Shutterstock.com; pp. 3-32 swissdrone/Shuttertock.com; p.5 Logvin art/Shutterstock.com; pp. 5, 11, 15, 17, 19, 25. Cal Sport Media / Alamy Stock Photo; pp. 3, 4, 5, 6, 10,12, 14, 18, 26, 28, 30, 31, 32 Dadan Andriyana/Shutterstock.com; pp. 5, 7, 16, 20, 22, 24 Kovalov Anatolii/Shutterstock.com; pp. 5,6, 8, 11, 13, 15, 16, 19, 21,22, 24, 27, 28, 30 MamasOmar/Shutterstock.com; p. 5 Oleksandr Poliashenko/Shutterstock.com; p. 7 ASSOCIATED PRESS; p .9 Jamie Lamor Thompson/Shutterstock.com; p. 13 Kevin Williams / Alamy Stock Photo; p. 21, 27 Zuma Press, Inc. / Alamy Stock Photo; p. 23 April Visuals/Shutterstock.com; p. 29 UPI / Alamy Stock Photo.

Printed in the United States of America

CPSIA compliance information: Batch #CSGS26: For further information contact Gareth Stevens, at 1-800-542-2595.

CONTENTS

PRESCOTT'S PRESENCE

Dak Prescott has a great arm and is a leader on the field. At every level of football, from high school to college to the National Football League (NFL), Prescott has been a game-changing quarterback. His ambition, or drive, started young and continues today!

NATHANIEL PRESCOTT

Prescott's family didn't have much while he was growing up. Sometimes they didn't even have a home. Still, Prescott knew he was meant for greatness. He said he would grow up to be a movie star, the U.S. president, or an NFL superstar.

IN THE POCKET

WITH PRESCOTT AND HIS BROTHERS, EVERYTHING WAS A CONTEST, OR GAME. THEY HAD ROLLERBLADING RACES AND OREO-EATING CONTENTS!

GAME
EXPERIENCE
ATL Royalty
MAXIM
EXPERIENCES
AMUZE
AKG
HARMAN
BLENDED SCOTCH
WAFFLE
HOUSE
APEX
SOCIAL CLUB @ PALMS
ROOFTOP2
PRODUCTIONS

HIGH SCHOOL STAR

Prescott took over as quarterback of his high school team when the starting quarterback got injured, or hurt. In his final year of high school, he led the team to the **quarterfinals** of the state championships but lost. In 2011, Prescott began playing football for the Mississippi State University Bulldogs.

IN THE POCKET

PRESCOTT'S HIGH SCHOOL FOOTBALL TEAM DIDN'T LOSE ANY GAMES IN THE 2010 REGULAR SEASON!

STARTING AT STATE

Prescott redshirted his first year at Mississippi State. In the 2012 season, Prescott played quarterback in 12 games. He scored his first touchdown for Mississippi State in the first game of the season. He went on to score seven more touchdowns that season!

IN THE POCKET

REDSHIRT MEANS TO SIT OUT OF GAMES FOR A YEAR. THIS LETS COLLEGE STUDENTS PLAYING SPORTS KEEP FOUR YEARS OF ELIGIBILITY WHILE STILL PRACTICING WITH THE TEAM.

BREAKING RECORDS

In 2013, Prescott became the starting quarterback after another quarterback got hurt. That season, Prescott broke the Mississippi State record for most rushing yards in one season by a quarterback with 829. He was named **MVP** in the Liberty Bowl too.

IN THE POCKET

PRESCOTT'S MOM DIED OF CANCER IN 2013. HE HAS HONORED HER MEMORY IN MANY WAYS, INCLUDING RAISING MONEY FOR CANCER RESEARCH.

Prescott began the 2014 season as the starting quarterback for Mississippi State. He led the team to the school's first-ever number one **ranking**! He also broke 10 school records that season, including the most single season passing yards at 3,449.

IN THE POCKET

PRESCOTT STUDIED PSYCHOLOGY, OR THE STUDY OF THE MIND AND HOW PEOPLE ACT, AT MISSISSIPPI STATE. HE CHOSE THIS SO HE COULD BECOME A GOOD COACH SOMEDAY.

MISSISSIPPI
STATE
SEC
15
93

MISSISSIPPI #GREAT

Prescott's play in 2015 put him in the top quarterbacks of all time in the Southeastern Conference (SEC) for rushing yards and touchdowns. This made it likely he'd be **drafted** into the NFL. It also helped improve, or better, Mississippi State's football program as a whole!

IN THE POCKET

DAN MULLEN, THE HEAD COACH OF MISSISSIPPI STATE, SAID PRESCOTT "MIGHT BE THE BEST PLAYER I'VE EVER COACHED."

COWBOYS BALL

The Dallas Cowboys chose Prescott in the 2016 NFL Draft. He was picked 135th overall. Prescott was going to be the third in line to play quarterback for the Cowboys. At the time, the team had a superstar quarterback in Tony Romo.

IN THE POCKET

PRESCOTT'S ABILITIES WERE UNDERESTIMATED IN THE 2016 DRAFT. IN FACT, SEVEN OTHER QUARTERBACKS WERE CHOSEN AHEAD OF HIM!

At Cowboys training camp, a player injury allowed Prescott to have a chance at being Romo's backup. Then, Romo got hurt during the preseason. Prescott went on to start all 16 regular season games for the Cowboys in the 2016–2017 season!

IN THE POCKET

PRESCOTT CAME IN AS THE STARTING QUARTERBACK FOR THE COWBOYS IN THE 2017–2018 SEASON. HIS TEAM CHOSE HIM TO BE A CAPTAIN TOO!

In 2018, Prescott led the Cowboys to an NFC East championship. The following season, Prescott and the Cowboys finished with eight wins and eight losses. Prescott became only the second Cowboy's quarterback in history to throw for more than 4,000 yards in a season!

IN THE POCKET

PRESCOTT HAD A FOOTBALL FIELD PUT IN AT HIS HOME OUTSIDE DALLAS, TEXAS.

INJURY AND COMING BACK

After just five games in 2020, Prescott hurt his ankle badly. That ended the season for him. He came back in 2021 to throw for 37 touchdowns! After the 2022 season, Prescott was named the Walter Payton Man of the Year, honoring his community service as well as on-field play.

IN THE POCKET

PRESCOTT HAS WORKED WITH MENTAL HEALTH GROUPS; DONATED, OR GIVEN, THOUSANDS OF MEALS TO THOSE WITHOUT HOMES; AND MORE.

FUTURE GOAT?

Prescott and the Cowboys finished the 2023–2024 season 12–5 . They still didn't make a deep playoff run. An injury in November 2024 ended Prescott's season—but it's clear not much can stop him! What will he accomplish next?

IN THE POCKET

PRESCOTT SIGNED A FOUR-YEAR, $240 MILLION DEAL WITH THE COWBOYS IN 2021. IT WAS THE BIGGEST DEAL IN TEAM HISTORY TO THAT POINT.

DAK PRESCOTT'S FOOTBALL TIMELINE

2007	Prescott starts playing football for Haughton High School.
2010	His high school team doesn't lose any games in the regular season.
2011	He starts playing for Mississippi State University. He redshirts his first season.
2013	He becomes the starting quarterback for Mississippi State.
2014	He breaks 10 Mississippi State football records.
2016	The Dallas Cowboys draft him. He starts all 16 regular season games.
2018	The Cowboys win the NFC East championship.
2021	He signs a huge four-year deal with the Cowboys.
2023	He is named the Walter Payton Man of the Year.

FOR MORE INFORMATION

BOOKS

Leed, Percy. *Meet the Dallas Cowboys*. Minneapolis, MN: Lerner Publications, 2026.

Morey, Allan. *Dak Prescott*. Minneapolis, MN: Bellwether Media, 2023.

Roland, James. *The Next Generation: NFL Star Quarterbacks*. San Diego, CA: ReferencePoint Press, 2025.

WEBSITES

Dak Prescott—Mississippi State
https://hailstate.com/sports/football/roster/dak-prescott/2911
See the many awards Prescott won in college and read more about his career at Mississippi State.

Dak Prescott—ESPN
https://www.espn.com/nfl/player/_/id/2577417/dak-prescott
Stay up to date on Prescott's play with the Dallas Cowboys on ESPN.com.

GLOSSARY

cancer: A disease caused by the uncontrolled growth of cells in the body.

draft: To be selected from a pool of potential players entering the league. Also, the process of selecting new players.

eligibility: Having to do with being qualified to do something.

MVP: Most valuable, or best, player.

quarterfinals: In a tournament, the four games that decide which four of the eight teams left will go on.

ranking: The standing within a group.

research: Study to learn something new.

underestimate: To place a lower value on someone than they should have.

INDEX